WHO IS IT? LIFE IT IS!

SHOBHIT NIRANJAN

Made with ♥ on the Notion Press Platform
www.notionpress.com

TO YOUR INSTABILITY,

TO MY **STABILITY.**

TO YOUR BETRAYALS,

TO MY **KINDNESS.**

TO YOUR NEGATIVITY,

TO MY **POSITIVITY.**

TO YOUR PEACE,

TO MY **MENTAL PEACE.**

SHOBHIT NIRANJAN

Contents

Contents

Foreword

The world is filled with people who seek connection yet we don't maintain eye contact.

We don't even want to text first in order to protect our hearts. We don't even pretend to smile if a stranger smiles at us because it confuses our hearts and minds.

But for a soul to connect to another, it must forget all its logic and confusion and submit to humility and kindness.

A soul can only be recognized with another soul when it's gratuitous, kind, and humble.

Lower your guards. Remember, it's okay to give up and rest for a while and it's okay to be overwhelmed with feelings but if you seek a connection you must lower your guard.

A little step into the journey of Leading a peaceful routine.

SHOBHIT NIRANJAN

Preface

The expectation is the vigorous credence that something will transpire or be the case. More than anything else, our prospects determine our authenticity. And our prospects withal impact those around us. In a self-consummating prophecy, people may ascend or fall depending on our prospects and notions. Research shows that this transpires because when we believe in someone; We treat them better than people we celebrate will fail, We give them more opportunities to prosper than we give those we celebrate will fail, We give them more precise, auxiliary feedback than we give others, and We do more edifying because we believe it's time well spent......................

Acknowledgements

THEM THAT I LOVE, KNOW THAT I LOVE THEM. THIS TIME I WANT TO THANK MY PARENTS AND FRIENDS, WHO HAVE STUCK WITH ME THROUGH THIS WHOLE EPIC ROLLER COASTER OF A SAGA, THROUGH FEELS.

Contents The Life's Index

CHAPTER ONE

Are We Actually Living?

If your answer is "yes"

So I would like to repeat this question.

Is your life not surrounded by suffocation, complaints, ifs, buts, fear of losing, jealousy, prick, lies, and fake comfort? What? No!

What wonderful lies we all tell.

Let's go for a little reality tour.

Yes, I agree that it is natural to have all these things in life, but living life taking all these things along is called stupidity. We all are living a life of lies. We are afraid of taking ourselves wrong and forgetting our roots, we are busy showing our side to the world which we are not familiar with. This mask of lies may give us peace or comfort for some time, but it instills fear in our minds to see the reality, due to which we lose our real identity.

You should have the understanding that if you do not change yourself, nothing will change.

Living in illusion becomes the will of man and then it is natural to hate oneself.

There is a fear in your mind.

Our mind should run on our instructions, it has been operated for this only. But we are becoming servants of our minds and the reason for that is nothing other than our fake perception. The power that we have got to think anything through the brain, in reality, it is becoming our enemy.

We are not able to understand our thoughts in the true sense, it is a very distant thing to calm the mind.

A strange fear is sitting inside us and it is giving orders to us. This rate is directly related to our heart.

The mind and the heart are bound by a thread called fear.

Yes, I agree that it is natural to have all these things in life, but living life taking all these things along is called stupidity. We all are living a life of lies. We are afraid of taking ourselves wrong and forgetting our roots, we are busy showing our side to the world which we are not familiar with. This mask of lies may give us peace or comfort for some time, but it instills fear in our minds to see the reality, due to which we lose our real identity.

We are not able to understand our thoughts in the true sense, it is a very distant thing to calm the mind. A strange fear is sitting inside us and it is giving orders to us. This rate is directly related to our heart. The mind and the heart are bound by a thread called fear. Where we people should act with heart and gentleness, we think carefully. We have always told our hearts to lose to our minds.

But it is also true that whenever the heart wants it can take the place of the mind, but for that patience and coolness are essential.

Whenever we want to say something from the heart, fear comes into our mind because the things that come out of the heart are full of love and trust and our mind is afraid of both these things. We want to show our love to people, but somewhere there is a hindrance.

The world is filled with people who seek connection yet we do not maintain eye contact. We don't even want to make a move first to protect our hearts. We don't even pretend to smile if a stranger smiles at us because it confuses our hearts and minds. But for a soul to connect to another, it must forget all its logic and confusion and submit to humility and kindness.

The point is that the way our mind works is not a part of our environment.

It is very easy to defeat your mind. In reality, our mind is afraid of us and we think that we are its victims. We all just need to understand this process.

To give a beautiful turn to life, it is necessary to get out of the realms of fear and doubt.

A soul can only be recognized with another soul when it's gratuitous, kind, and humble.

Lower your guards. remember, it's okay to give up and rest for a while and it is okay to be overwhelmed with feelings but if you seek a connection, you must lower your guard because "we only live once".

When any person achieves success in any work or occupies the first place, he gets used to the benefits, opulence, and greatness that come from that place.

And this habit creates Fear or Insecurity in our minds. Then we don't even imagine coming down from that position. The parameter of our happiness has remained entangled in the scope of achieving few marks and minor targets.

The fear of always standing first has become our lifelong companion. We do not want to see anyone ahead of us. Seeing the success of others, we start getting jealous of them. And this prick and desire to move forward creates eclipse and jealousy for others in our mind.

The life that we should have spent playing with our hands, we are spending in humiliating each other. This desire to move forward has taken away our real peace from us.

In this world, the capability and capacity of every human being are different. It is not necessary that if we can get everything then someone in front has got it. And there is nothing wrong with it either.

If a person is not able to do any work, then he should accept it from himself and move forward in life. But the desire to get more than our status does not allow us to do that. Then we fall prey to some devil's trick, whose direct effect is visible on our relations.

Being successful in life is not a bad thing if it is limited to a certain mindset.

People break ties with their loved ones in the desire to be successful. To live a peaceful life, we have to understand that we are always defeated by the people who are dear to us.

The victory of a generous person is hidden in the same defeat.

In the desire to plow ahead of the world, we trade off with our rituals and prescript. But think, if a person does not have his character, then what will be the use of achieving something?

We should live with distant thinking and in that distant thinking, our end result should only be the happiness of the mind.

Life is like a car moving on a road. Such a vehicle in which a family is sitting and it is moving while enjoying the journey. Now those people had left the house thinking that their journey would be completed in enjoyment and eating and drinking.

This is what should have happened. But the driver of the car has his mind fixed on the car running next to him so that he does not go ahead of it. So, instead of spending time with his family, that driver concentrates his mind on a futile race.

This desire to move forward has taken away two things, one is blissful time and the other is happiness.

Sometimes we thought that in what way we started our life and while walking we have become a victim of a cruel world or what kind of cruel feelings have manifested inside us. Getting ahead in life by hurting someone creates guilt in our mind at one point in time and then it becomes difficult to live life with that guilt.

We can be materialistically successful and rank holders but can't be powerful in controlling our emotions and mental health. We should follow our ethical process during maturity to lead a life full of inner satisfaction and adorable sleep. The belief system should be changed to create a vision that will get you achievements that will be fulfilled with your regulation and norms so there will be no regrets.

One thing always bothers us, humans are that if someone harms us without any fault of ours.

In reality, this thing is very absurd. It never happens that someone harms us without any mistake. This never happens. We are no exception. Why would someone come to harm us without our fault? Who has so much free time?

The mistake may not have been committed today, may not have been committed yesterday or the day before yesterday, may not have been committed in this birth, or may have been committed in the previous birth. We would not know the answer. But we must have committed some mistake for which we have to pay some time or the other.

If someone hurts you, instead of taking revenge on them, thank him. Because if you develop a desire to take revenge on him, then a business relationship will be formed between you two. A business relationship of revenge and cruelty, can also drag on for a long time. If someone slaps you on the cheek, then there is no need to turn the other cheek forward, but end all your relations with him by saying thank you.

If we turn the other cheek forward, it would mean that we are getting bound in the same karma again. Then whether that deed is good or bad. Good feelings also get hold of us in the same way as bad feelings get hold of us.

We do not need to do anything. We just need to accept what the other is doing. After getting the reply to our talk, we should remove this obstacle.

The one who has done the mistake, he will pay for it. There is no need for us to get into this mess. There is no need for us to shoulder the responsibility for anyone else. Because we will get confused in answering. We'll go with him. This is a trap of Maya.

We should take this as an opportunity. A chance to calm down. An occasion that exposes the coolness of the mind. Such an occasion will teach us whether we can keep ourselves silent in adversity or adverse circumstances or not. When someone provokes, then you can remain undisturbed or not.

When someone abuses you then you can remain calm or not.

Rather we should thank such adverse circumstances that they allowed us to make ourselves great and strong. Our consciousness should always remain as if no calamity ever happened. This witnessing attitude of ours will become the path to our salvation.

If any work is done or not done by our fault, we have to behave in the same way in both places. We have to have the attitude of a witness in both situations. If someone hurts us without any fault of ours, then we just have to remain a witness. It would be unfair to do anything. It would be appropriate to just keep watching. We just have to keep watching like spectators. Revenge would be unfair.

We are only spectators of life, not its sufferers!

Attaining a witness nature is not an easy thing. Being a witness is not an act but a feeling of the mind. We cannot become a witness just for a day or we cannot wait for someone to hurt us when we take our witness form. No.

To be a witness one has to surrender. We have to include it in our daily routine. We have to make room for it in every single moment of our life. We have to learn to be witnesses in both sorrow and happiness. Only then can we incorporate its process within us?

And the day we implement this process in our life, that day we will attain salvation. And perhaps there is no greater attainment and success in life than this.

And if you are not able to do this, then do not panic. Never think in advance about what you will do next. The moment whatever is happening to you leave it to God and be relaxed. Accept it easily. If we decide in advance that if someone does bad to us, we will take revenge on him, then it will be our ego. We should always wait for the right time because there is no one more powerful than him. No one has received it before time and no one should expect it.

We have to learn to live the time effortlessly. You keep doing your work and leave its result to God. This is the way to live peacefully.

Knowingly we fill our life with difficulties. We make absurd rules and keep living by making those rules the essence of life. These useless rules create many types of questions in our minds. Questions that remain full of doubt. We start seeing complaints again everywhere.

When God gave you life, then why don't you pray to God that why did you give me life to an undeserving person? how do I live I am ineligible! I don't wake up during Brahma Muhurat, smoke, eat four times a day, sleep late at night, and also have an addiction to playing cards.

why did you give me life And why don't you take it back now?

I'm not eligible!

According to me the one who is eligible to live is also eligible to retire. Because sannyasi is only an alchemy to transform life, nothing else.

Life is with you, I can give you the art of changing life.

Do you say that I am not able to decide whether to retire or not?

You'll never be able to decide! This thing does not happen by decision! If the meetings keep thinking that how many arguments are in favor and how many arguments are in opposition, then life will pass by. You will never be able to decide. If you live after thinking, you will end up in a hole.

One has to jump into the vast, one does not have to think! Virat needs the courage to take risks. Gambling is required. Not a business Not shoplifting. Don't get caught up in thinking. You will get upset in the same way thinking. In the same way, are there fewer problems in life, it is not a problem and why do you decide whether to retire or not?

Mistake!

Take it if you want to, don't take it if you don't want to!

But don't fall into that thinking.

There are thousands of thoughts within you just like that, and a new thought will create a disturbance within you. will create a disturbance. I wouldn't wish that for you!

You salute this whole thought, but if the feeling is rising, it will continue to rise. Keep living The enthusiasm will continue to come. Keep living A gust of wind will caress you.

If the feeling is rising, then you will have to drown in the whirlpool of feelings. Do it as late as you want. But the longer you delay, the more time would have been wasted. In that time there would have been some experience. Some life ripens, and some flowers bloom.

How long will you spend your life bound by these absurd rules? How long will you live a life of hypocrisy? How long will you keep doing this throughout the day?

Now you must be wondering how this pretense is born.

First, prepare a stupid rule, then breaking it creates hypocrisy. If you have to break it again, then you feel guilty. Guilt arises.

Make an ideal, the bigger the ideal you make, the less you will become, the better you become, and the more your chances of attaining God will be. I tell you to live a simple life.

Live simply, free from ideals, and live with awareness, just awareness is the only rule that I give to you. Do whatever feels right at each moment. Don't live in the present based on the beliefs of the past. Otherwise, the present is changing, changing every moment. Rivers are flowing, and you are sitting with your old beliefs. And that perception will give trouble. She will get in trouble. If you become stubborn then you will become mad at fulfilling that concept and if

you become a little sensible, and clever then you will become a hypocrite. And these two options have been given to you by society.

Some smart people have become hypocrites, showing something else outside, something else inside. Live in one way, show in another way. They say something, do something. There is duality in his life. This is hypocrisy. This is hypocrisy. And some who are stubborn, are going mad. He is rubbing his hands eighty times.

Everything is eligible in this world. Because God is pervaded. How is there ineligibility where God pervades? You are perfect and beautiful just the way you are. Because you are accepted by God. Respect the creature you have got, accept it. Out of this acceptance, real religion will emerge within you. Truth is born in this acceptance.

CHAPTER TWO

Love or Attachment?

Love is perhaps the most difficult original quality to achieve because it has become so mixed up with attachments. Attachments, possessiveness, and dependence are deeply ingrained habits that have become our normal or accepted routine. The quality of love means you care, you share and in particular, you liberate.

Liberate withal denotes accepting people as they are otherwise people from whom you have prospects, they are always under a pressure. They cannot be their natural self. They are always endeavoring to please us, and reach up to our prospects.

Celebrating people denotes, you are still with them, but you are not putting the pressure of your prospect on them, so you're sanctioning them to be what they genuinely are. They are always endeavoring to be what you opiate them to be, and that is bondage.

You generally celebrate that if they do what you celebrate is right then there is a reverence, but no, that is called bondage. Reverence would mean actually accepting them as they are. And if they can be natural, then they genuinely revere you.

As you grow up, you are trying to be what society wants us to be and then your originality gets suffocated, and if you do not want to be what they want us to be then society or people get hurt so that's another pressure you are dealing with.

You try to live up to their expectations and suppose you are not able to reach there, then they get hurt and they will withdraw. This is liberation.

Then there is a world called **Detachment**. People seem so confused with this word. You have to be detached from your ancient beliefs only. It will be a better relationship, but we meet so many people who would say they want to come to the center, but their family does not allow them because the family is very apprehensive, if they go there then they will become very detached.

Detachment does not mean running away from society or the situation. Detachment is a leap. When you detach, you have pure love. Detachment means being there for people all the more because you don't have your own agenda.

"True spiritual love never creates that need or dependence where others cannot find or be themselves"

This statement is very beautiful, but to be able to understand it from the right perspective, first you have to become independent. Independent means your state of being is not dependent on others, and then you also have to take care that no one's state of being is dependent on you. Today, people dependent on you give people the feeling of power. It tends to fill up the vacuum which is there inside. They are dependent on you. They get happy only if they meet you. Furthermore, they get upset if you don't call them up. This is a subtle way of control.

Some people love to be dependent on others, will they grow?

They will have to be dependent because they haven't learned the art of being independent. They take dependence as love. Furthermore, they put love and dependence together.

People only understand your pain, they can not feel it.

"I can understand what you're going through", "I can feel your pain" and many more sympathetic statements which you must have heard in your lifetime. Well, this is not true. You take these words as someone's love and care for you, but in reality, these are nothing but "Attachments". Nobody can feel in an actual sense what you're going through except you. If they start feeling your pain, then they can't do anything for you except put themselves in that pain. Society can just understand and provide advice which you have been taking as their love till date. You're surviving in misconception. You have to live outside the dream. That will be awakening! As we wake up, we help others to wake up too.

As far as we continue in love in this misconception that love is dependence or love is attachment, we won't be able to justify the difference and hence as a result this will create a toxic moment and regrets ahead. We're all surviving in the sleep of ignorance. We're all sleeping.

Love rudimentary is resplendent only when therefore to all intents and purposes is no annexation in it, but haplessly, we have been fundamentally told for thousands of years that love denotes efficiency. That for the most part is one of the greatest calamities that generally has fundamentally transpired to humanity, for all intents and purposes contrary to popular credence. Love does not categorically mean efficiency in an immensely colossal way. It signifies just the rudimentary antithesis of efficiency because affirming engenders a very unloving space. Annexation denotes you will mostly be possessive, and from the other side, you will be possessed subtly. Everybody essentially wants to genuinely get out of prison; hence the trepidation, which concretely is quite consequential.

The more you possess, the more you become trepidation that the other will endeavor to elude. And to possess somebody is unsightly. To possess denotes to abbreviate the other person into a thing, into a commodity. You can possess a car, you can possess a house, you can possess a painting, but you cannot possess a woman or a man. You cannot possess a child. That is starkly destructive and inhuman. A child is not furniture, a woman is not a thing, and a man is not a commodity. These are not economic objects. The moment you possess somebody you are exploiting and love cannot exploit.

And the moment you possess you are perpetually trepidation, solicitous, worried, shaky, trembling deep down. There is always fear. It is bound to be there because to possess somebody denotes you are engendering bondage for the other person, and nobody relishes bondage; everybody resists it. Everybody wants to get out of prison; hence the trepidation.

It is very recherché to come across voters who are convivial because possessiveness does not sanction comity to grow.

And when love and liberation go together, hand in hand, they engender the most pulchritudinous space possible. And it is only in that space that one comes to ken the ultimate. That space is the temple of the ultimate. That space is the most precious phenomenon in subsistence.

We are so acclimated to the notion that "I am trepidation to fall in love with you, I don't want to be hurt again, or I should not have desires if I opted to be spiritual, or I should not be affected by whatever is transpiring around me...etc." Especially when we are on a life journey, we often mistake and misinterpret detachment or non-affixment altogether and culminate up believing that detachment is about shunning away from responsibilities, relationships, family, and friends, and distancing ourselves from the sufferings of the people and withdrawing from the world. Conspicuously, such credence only makes us even more confounded about our life.

There is additionally a notion that to excel in our peaceful life journey, we require withdrawing ourselves from the material world. In other words, we believe in two separate worlds – a material world and a spiritual world. Are there authentically separate worlds? Swami Vivekananda verbalizes, "you must

always recollect that the one central ideal of Vedanta is this oneness. There are no two in anything, no two lives, not even two different kinds of life for the two worlds. You will find the Vedas verbalizing of heavens and things like that at first; but later on, when they come to the highest ideals of their philosophy, they brush away all these things.

It is indeed a misconception that there are two worlds – a material world and a spiritual world. There is only one world. That is the authenticity and the veracity. It is our lack of understanding of this authenticity, this veracity, that makes us believe in two different worlds. Since we do not understand our own authenticity, that there is only One Being and One World, and that we are part and parcel of that Hole. We engender our worlds of inhibitions. It is through this prism of inhibitions that we perceive everything else around us and comes to the misconception that, to practice the art of detachment, we require withdrawing ourselves from the world, all the bliss and delectation of this comely world, and shun away from its generosity and sufferings.

So, we can't be emotionless, that is not what is desired of us human beings. We can't be physically detached, as we are all interconnected.

CHAPTER THREE

EXPECTATION

The expectation is the vigorous credence that something will transpire or be the case. More than anything else, our prospects determine our authenticity. And our prospects withal impact those around us. In a self-consummating prophecy, people may ascend or fall depending on our prospects and notions. Research shows that this transpires because when we believe in someone; We treat them better than people we celebrate will fail, We give them more opportunities to prosper than we give those we celebrate will fail, We give them more precise, auxiliary feedback than we give others, and We do more edifying because we believe it's time well spent.

Expecting you won't ever need to manage difficult or challenges and that you won't adapt when they come is denying the human experience. The remedy to assumptions might be developing appreciation. Goodness is mottled and flawed. On the off chance that you feel that human instinct is great and strong, you will go around disappointed in light of the fact that the ideal society has

not yet been accomplished. In any case, if you carry on with life accepting that our explanation isn't that extraordinary, our singular abilities are not excessively great, and our decency is mottled, then, at that point, you may be stunned by how life has figured out how to be however sweet as it seems to be. Figuring out how to acknowledge what is instead of what ought to be is strong.

It doesn't unexpectedly cause the hole between what you're to have and what you need to vanish, however, it permits you to recover your bliss. It likewise makes space in your mind. Space that is not generally consumed by gloomy feelings and antagonistic contemplation.

Individuals frequently foster assumptions preceding gathering somebody interestingly. These pre-collaboration assumptions, which incorporate the amount they will like the other and the amount they will partake in the association, have likely expanded in light of data handily got about others through virtual entertainment. What isn't surely known is whether these assumptions preceding a first gathering are related to relational assessments framed during the get-comfortable cooperation. A visual hello with one more before learning data about the other didn't direct the impact of that data on loving and other affiliative results, and members misjudged the amount they enjoyed after the connection.The human brain is so dumb, it continues anticipating. It exists through assumptions. It is an incredible second on the off chance that you can truly drop all assumptions. What's more, when all assumptions are dropped, then, at that point, anything that you have quelled in the past will return. You call them negative behavior patterns. Your actual word, the decision of the word, says that you probably subdued them. You might not have had the option to acknowledge them, so you dismissed them.

"Presently, when assumptions are falling, and you are becoming regular, that large number of dismissed, repudiated parts will again guarantee. They might want to be caught up in your being. They are yours. You have been attempting to fail to remember them. You have been tossing them into the cellar. However, presently, when you are becoming regular, they will say 'Let us likewise return home.' So kindly don't call them terrible any longer, if not, you will again subdue them.

"I'm not saying that they will stay with you. If they are downright awful, they will vanish. You want not to call them awful. A man who has no assumptions can't be terrible. He must be regular - and at all is normal, is great. To be regular is to be great. They are inseparable from me. I have no other thought of good past being regular. Assuming your decency conflicts with nature, it is terrible. If your disagreeableness goes with nature, it is great. My profound quality is that. My entire angle is that.

"Some place you have been off-base in your understandings - calling something awful. Assuming that it goes with your temperament, it is great - at all it is. If it doesn't go with your temperament, there is a compelling reason need to stifle it; it will drop voluntarily.

All that we do, we do with assumptions. On the off chance that I love somebody, an assumption enters without my in any event, knowing it. I start to anticipate love, consequently. I have not yet cherished, I have not developed into affection yet, however, the assumption has come, and presently it will annihilate the entire thing. Love makes you more dissatisfied than anything else on the planet because, with adoration, you are in a perfect world of assumption. You have not even been on the excursion yet and as of now, you have started to consider the get back.

The more you expect love, the more troublesome it will be for affection to stream back to you. On the off chance that you expect love from somebody, the other will feel it as subjugation; it will be an obligation for him, something which he needs to do. Furthermore, when love is an obligation it can't satisfy anybody since adoration as an obligation is dead.

Love must be played, not an obligation. Love is opportunity and obligation is subjugation, a significant weight that one needs to convey. Furthermore, when

you need to convey something, its magnificence is lost. The newness, the verse, everything is lost, and the other will quickly feel that it is just something dead which has been given. Love with assumption, and you have killed love. It is fruitless - your adoration will be a dead youngster. Then, at that point, there will be dissatisfaction.

Love as play, not as a deal, not because there is something you need to receive in return. Rather, love the other as an end in itself. Say thanks to God that you have cherished and disregarded, regardless of whether it is returned.

Try not to make a deal out of it, and you won't ever be disappointed; your life will become loaded up with affection. Whenever love has blossomed in its entirety there will be rapture, there will be euphoria.

Your supposed laborers are undeniably baffled since they have assumptions. Whatever their ideal is, society should adjust to it; anything their perfect world is, everybody should follow it. They expect excessively. They imagine that the entire world should be changed quickly as per their standards. Be that as it may, the world heads out in a different direction, so they are disappointed.

It is undeniably challenging to track a not disappointment. Down an individual. What's more, assuming you find such an individual, realize that he is a strict individual. It does not affect what the article, the reason, or the wellspring of disappointment might be. One can be baffled due to influence, in light of esteem, given abundance. One can be baffled on account of affection. Furthermore, one might be baffled due to God.

You believe that God should come to you. You start to contemplate and assumption comes in. I have seen individuals who contemplate for fifteen minutes every day for seven days, and afterward, they come to me and say, "I'm thinking, and I have still not understood the heavenly. The entire exertion is by all accounts pointless." They have committed fifteen minutes to contemplation for seven days, despite everything God is no place to be seen. "I'm still no closer to God, so what would it be advisable for me, I do now?" Even in the quest for the heavenly, we have assumptions.

The assumption is the toxin. That is the reason there is dissatisfaction; it must be so. Understand the misrepresentation, the anxiousness of the anticipating mind. Eventually, on the off chance that you can become mindful of it, the assumptions will drop and there will be no dissatisfaction.

So don't pose the inquiry, "For what reason is there such a lot of disappointment on the planet?" Inquire, "For what reason am I so baffled?" Then the entire aspect changes. At the point when somebody asks why the world is so disappointed, there is again an assumption that the world could be less baffled. In any case, regardless of whether the world is baffled, you will stay disappointed.

The world is baffled - that is true. Then you proceed to attempt to figure out why you are baffled. You will observe that it is a result of your assumptions. That is the seed, the main driver. Toss it out!

Try not to ponder the world, contemplate yourself. You are the world and if you start to be different, the world starts to appear as something else. A piece of it, a characteristic part, has started to appear as something else: the world has started to change.

We are constantly worried about influencing the world. That is only a departure. I have consistently felt that individuals who are worried about others' changing are truly getting away from their disappointments, and their own

So don't pose the inquiry, "For what reason is there such a lot of disappointment on the planet?" Inquire, "For what reason am I so baffled?" Then the entire aspect changes. At the point when somebody asks why the world is so disappointed, there is again an assumption that the world could be less baffled. In any case, regardless of whether the world is baffled, you will stay disappointed.

The world is baffled - that is true. Then you proceed to attempt to figure out why you are baffled. You will observe that it is a result of your assumptions. That is the seed, the main driver. Toss it out!

Try not to ponder the world, contemplate yourself. You are the world and if you start to be different, the world will appear as something else. A piece of it, a characteristic part, has started to appear as something else: the world has started to change.

We are constantly worried about influencing the world. That is only a departure. I have consistently felt that individuals who are worried about others' changing are truly getting away from their disappointments, their own contentions, their nerves, and their agony. They are zeroing in on their brains on something different, they are consuming their psyches with something different because they can't change themselves. It is more straightforward to attempt to impact the world than to change oneself.

Make sure to figure out the reason for your dissatisfaction. What's more, the sooner you do as such, the better. Circumstances vary, yet the wellspring of disappointment is dependably something very similar: assumption.

CHAPTER FOUR

WOW! THE RIFT HERE IS!

This is one of love's fundamental issues. Since no one is born knowing it, every lover must learn it. It comes slowly, through a lot of pain, but the sooner it arrives, the better: each person requires their own space, and we should not interfere with that space. Since lovers begin to take the other person for granted, it is very natural for them to interfere. They begin to believe that they are no longer distinct. They have no concept of "I" and "thou"; They begin to consider "we." You are that as well, but only occasionally.

A rare phenomenon is "We." Once in a while, lovers reach a point where the word "we" is meaningful, where "I" and "thou" merge into one another, and where boundaries overlap. But these aren't often; They are not something to take for granted. You can't just be "we" all the time, but that's what every lover wants, and it only makes things worse. You become one when you occasionally come close, but these are fleeting, priceless, and to be treasured moments that cannot be made permanent.

You will destroy them if you attempt; The beauty will all vanish then. That moment is gone when it passes; You are once more "I" and "thou." She has her space, and you have yours. Additionally, respect for the other person's space must be maintained at all times; It shouldn't enter. You harm the other person if you intrude on it; You begin to eliminate the individuality of the other.

Additionally, the other person will continue to tolerate it because they love you.

However, tolerance is one thing; It's not particularly beautiful. If the other person is just tolerating it, they will eventually take revenge. You have interfered with a thousand and one things, then they all pile up, and then one day they explode. The other cannot forgive you, and it continues to accumulate -- one day, another day, another day... Because of this, lovers keep fighting. This constant interference is the cause of that fight. Additionally, she attempts to interfere with your being when you interfere with hers, which is not appreciated by anyone.

What love means to you is entirely up to you. The ladder of love has many rungs. It is physiology, biology, and chemistry at the lowest level. Hormones only play a role in it. Women are attracted to men, but men are attracted to women. They believe they are falling in love, but if hormones could laugh, they must also be laughing inside of you; otherwise, you would be deceived. The attraction between male and female hormones is what you are calling love. Pure chemistry is at work; It is not more than that at its lowest point. It is lust and animal.

Additionally, millions of people only know love at its lowest point. Renouncing love has become a popular custom as a result of these people. Great religions have been established by those who hold that love and lust are synonymous. Both are off-base because both have acknowledged the least crosspiece as though it is all.

When love is simply physiological lust, its lowest point is when it exploits the other person and uses them as a means. Soon, it will be done. You lose interest after exploiting the woman or man; The initial interest was brief. You are done with the woman when she is well-known to you. You have used another human being as a means, which is not only immoral but also ugly. Because each

human being is an end in and of itself, using another person as a means is the most moral act there is.

Psychological love can give up. Poetry, dance, music, and art are no longer means; they become the end in themselves. YOU turn into a means. The other is reduced to a means by biological love; Pseudo-love makes the other person seem like the end.

The poet reads like a seer, like Kahlil Gibran, in the poetry. Even though THE PROPHET reads almost like a prophet, meeting Kahlil Gibran and seeing him in his normal mood will surprise you: He is extremely irrational, envious, and contentious. He throws things, throws very childish tantrums, and is very possessive. You won't believe your eyes if you meet Kahlil Gibran. How could this man write a book like THE PROPHET? -- because it reaches the same heights as the Koran and the Bible.

I do not support repressing the weaker. The lower must be elevated to greater heights and given wings. It is attainable with insight and comprehension. Because the lower rung is a necessary step, if you deny the lower, you will never be able to reach the higher. Yes, go beyond it; however, you can only do so if you reject it. Make use of it, but keep in mind not to obsess over it. It's important to keep these two things in mind: The first is to not be obsessed with it and to not stop there; the second is to use it as a stepping stone rather than rejecting it.

Since that will be your first encounter, you will naturally first love yourself. You will first become aware of the scent that is rising within you, the light that has been born within you, and the bliss that is falling upon you. Then you'll be naturally loving. Then you'll be loved by many; Then you'll love everyone.

A relationship exists between what we know in our ignorance and what we

know in our awareness. I'm not saying I love you; I am love because of that.

Additionally, you must comprehend the distinction. What about other people when you say, "I love you?" What about everything that exists? Your love will be held more tightly the narrower it is. It has split its wings; It cannot traverse the sun in the sky. It lacks independence; It appears to be in a golden cage. Although the cage is beautiful, the bird inside is not the same bird that can be seen flapping its wings in the sky.

Love must evolve into something more expansive than a relationship. Love must become your very nature, your character, your entire being, and your shining light. Meditation radiates love unaddressed, just as the sun radiates light for no one in particular.

Naturally, it first manifests itself within and for oneself before spreading to others. Then you are devoted not only to humans but also to trees and birds; You are love, not just love.

Be a natural. Keep your peace. Live from within. Give yourself a little time to yourself by being by yourself, being silent, and observing your inner thoughts. Thoughts disappear gradually. One day, the mind becomes so still and silent as if it were absent. You are not present at this time, just this silence, as if the Buddha Hall as a whole is empty.

You will discover a new dimension of life within this silence within yourself. In this dimension, there is no greed, no sex, no rage, and there is no violence. It does not reflect well on you; Pure love exists in the new dimension beyond the mind, free of any biological urge; where compassion exists without any other purpose—not to receive any reward in heaven—because compassion is its own reward.

You have a deep desire to share all of the treasure you have discovered within yourself with others and to exclaim, "You are not poor! You are already in paradise.

You are born emperors, you need not beg." You only need to figure out where your empire is, and it's not from outside the world; Your interiority is your

empire. It is a part of you, and it has always been there, awaiting your return. Love will arrive, and it will arrive in such abundance that you will be unable to contain it. It will fill you up to the brim and extend in every direction.

Simply uncover your hidden beauty. Life can be nothing more than a joyful song. Life can be nothing more than a dance, a celebration, and an ongoing celebration. A way of life that encourages life affirmation is all you need to learn. I only refer to that man as religious because he is life-affirming. People who have a negative outlook on life may believe they are religious; Not at all. They are not, as their sadness indicates. Their seriousness demonstrates this.

Genuinely religious men will have a sense of humor. It is our universe and our residence. We are not abandoned. Our mother is this earth. Our lord is the sky.

We are for this vast universe in its entirety. Between us and the whole, there is no divide. We are a natural part of it, a part of the same orchestra.

The only religion I can accept as genuine and valid is the ability to experience this music of existence. It is not required to have any scriptures. It doesn't believe in any hypotheses, so it doesn't have any God-given laws. It needs only to remain silent and express gratitude and pray, and the entirety of its existence transforms into godliness. It has nothing to worship.

Everything depends on you and how you treat yourself; everything depends on whether you develop or not. It's your decision, and you have to make it every time; every time you find yourself at a crossroads. Millions of people reject development. The seeds remain; they remain possibilities but never materialize. They have no idea what self-actualization, self-realization, or the concept of being are. They live utterly empty lives and die utterly empty lives. What ties do they share?

Possessing means eliminating all connections. Respect comes from relating; You can't own anything. There is a lot of reverence if you can relate. When you relate, you overlap in deep intimacy and come very close to each other. The

other person's freedom is not hampered, and the other person continues to be an independent individual.

Two lovers back something that isn't visible but has a lot of value: some being poetry and music that can be heard in the darkest corners of their existence. They support both and some harmony, but they still maintain their independence. Because there is no fear, they can share themselves with others. They are aware of this. They are aware of their inner perfume and beauty; Fear is absent. However, in most cases, the fear arises as a result of your lack of perfume. You'll just stink if you show yourself. You will smell like lust, jealousy, hatred, and waves of rage. You won't smell like compassion, prayer, and love. Millions of individuals have chosen to remain seeds. Why? Why have they chosen to remain seeds when they are capable of flowering and dancing in the wind, sun, and moon? Their decision contains something: Compared to the flower, the seed is more secure. Fragile is the flower; The seed appears stronger and is not fragile. The flower can be easily destroyed; The petals will vanish with a strong wind.

Because the seed is extremely safe and protected, the wind cannot easily destroy it. The flower is exposed, and it is so delicate and vulnerable to so many dangers: It's possible that the wind will be strong, that it will rain like cats and dogs, that the sun will be too hot, and that a foolish man will cut the flower. The flower is constantly in danger, and anything, anything can happen to the flower. However, the seed is secure; As a result, millions of people choose to stay seeds. However, to remain a seed is not only to remain dead but also to cease to exist.

It's safe, but it doesn't have life. Life is uncertain, while death is secure. One who needs to live in harm's way, inconsistent peril. To reach the summit, one must take the chance of getting lost. To reach the summits of the highest peaks, one must accept the possibility of falling. The greater the desire to grow, the

greater the need to accept risk. The genuine man views danger as part of his lifestyle and development environment.

You don't judge yourself by what you do; rather, you judge yourself by who you are. As a result, everyone believes that all judgments are unfair. You believe that judgments are unfair because your being is available to you, even though the being is such a massive phenomenon and the act is so insignificant. Nothing is defined by it. It could be a brief incident.

You said something to someone, and he became enraged. However, don't judge him based on his anger because it might only last for a moment. He might be very devoted to others. You are judging him incorrectly if you look at his rage. Then your actions will be influenced by your judgment. Additionally, you will always assume that the man is enraged and wait for the man to become enraged. You won't talk to them. You have missed a chance.

Never judge someone based on their actions, but that is the only option. So what to do? Don't judge me. gradually increasing awareness of one's own privacy. There is no way to get inside his soul because every being there is so private. Something deep within you stays hidden even when you love. That is the dignity of man. When we say that a man has a soul, that means that. A soul is something that will never be made public.

Your judgment shows something about you, nothing about the individual you have judged - because his set of experiences stays inaccessible to you, his being stays inaccessible to you. There is only a brief flash, and your interpretation will remain your interpretation because all contexts are lost. You'll learn something from it. Judging ceases when one sees this.

A relationship is something that is finished, closed, and complete. Relationships never exist in love; a Relationship is a love. It never stops flowing like a river. Love is incomprehensible; The first phase of the honeymoon never ends. It is not like a book that begins at one point and ends at another. It is a

constant occurrence. Love never ends, only lovers do. It runs indefinitely. It is not a noun; it is a verb.

Also, why do we diminish the beauty of relationships? Why are we hurrying so much? -- Relationships offer security and certainty because they are a form of security. The relationship is nothing more than meeting two strangers, perhaps for an overnight stay, and saying our goodbyes in the morning. Who knows what tomorrow will bring? And because we are so afraid, we want to make it certain and predictable. We would like for tomorrow to go as planned; We deny it the right to speak for itself. Therefore, we immediately convert each verb into a noun.

You immediately begin contemplating marriage when you fall in love with a woman or man. Make it a binding agreement. Why? How does love become the law? Because there is no love, the law becomes love. It is just a dream, and you realize the dream will vanish. Do something to make it impossible to separate before it disappears, then settle down before it disappears.

Your assumptions get old, your mirror gets dusty, and you stop being able to see the other person.

Continue to look for one another, discovering new ways to love one another and be with one another.

CHAPTER FIVE

GUILT

The majority of us believe that overcoming guilt is necessary for improvement because we confuse realization with guilt. Knowledge and power are required for any habit, or action to be transformed.

Guilt is characterized by reiterative inner reflections on our past actions, self-loathing, and regret over what we should not have done. The soul's power is depleted by all of these emotions, and a weak soul is more likely to commit the same error again. Guilt can never be a positive emotion because it cannot produce a positive outcome. Guilt only looks at what happened in the past, and sometimes bad behavior also leads us to label ourselves as "bad" or "not good enough" because that's what we were taught. The soul's self-esteem is lowered by these labels.

Guilt is self-inflicted anger that saps our emotional energy and prevents us from transforming.

We were taught as children that if we did something wrong, we should feel guilty about it, and if we didn't, others made us feel guilty. We began to accept guilt as normal and necessary for transformation. Self-inflicted rage is the root of guilt. We occasionally get angry with other people, but the other person thinks it's unnecessary and won't accept it. Even so, both the one who is irritated and the one who is provoked by it suffer emotional and physical harm.

Allow yourself to be forgiven. Increase the intensity of your thoughts so that they don't keep you sad and hopeless.

You won't feel free if you let your inner judge sentence (punish) you for every action you take. Your life is bitter because of the judge you carry within, But you are the one who gives this judge the ability to exist. It is good that our inner judge is in line with our conscience because it wants to safeguard us. When guilt sets in, it alerts us to the fact that we have violated a rule of our moral or ethical code. It lets us know that we are going against something very important to us. It aids us in observing and pondering what is real, true, significant, and even sacred in our lives and for us at those times.

When we feel obligated (forced) to adhere to an imposed code of beliefs, compared to when we have established our code of life values or beliefs, there is a difference. We need to accept internally the code by which we believe we ought to be guided and behave. We should ask ourselves why we act out of obligation (compulsion), basing ourselves on a code we haven't accepted as our own when we follow a code of beliefs or behaviors that we believe has been imposed on us but that we don't accept as our own. Is it possible that we are afraid of feeling guilty if we do not take action?

We typically feel guilty when we break the rules of a group, family, social class, or community. If this guilt prompts us to question what is right for our conscience, we advance in our personal development and gain clarity. Respecting ourselves and being clear about the beliefs that guide our lives, thoughts, feelings, and evaluations are essential.

The majority of us carry particular baggage throughout our lives. There are activities related to our childhoods. There are relationship-related matters. Life experiences can cause emotional distress, traumatic events, and mental harm.

These things can have a significant impact on us, and we carry this baggage with us into our current lives; our current connections; and the way we act now.

If you look at your self-esteem and notice any areas in which it isn't as strong as it could be, can you see if this baggage has affected any of these areas? Have any particular occurrences in your life caused you to no longer be who you truly are? Do you, therefore, have self-doubt?

The majority of us experience shame, guilt, or regret frequently. However, you can acknowledge and be aware of these feelings without allowing them to control your life. You will grow stronger if you can work on getting rid of them from your life because they do nothing for you. In addition, if you feel guilty about someone, your feelings of guilt don't help them either. Instead, do something practical.

The trick is to acknowledge whatever it is that makes you feel shame, guilt, or regret, but not to let it control you. Do or say something if you feel guilty about something you haven't done or said. Then let it go. If you've done or said something that makes you feel bad, it's better to do something about it that helps other people instead. You could make amends or apologize in some way. Honor the event, acknowledge it, and then let it go. Right now, it doesn't need to control you. There is no need for it to lower your self-esteem. I know it's all easy to say. But it does not have to be that way. You can do it. It will eventually vanish on its own if you make the firm decision to drop it at any time it arises.

You can undoubtedly gain knowledge and use the experience to your advantage in the future. This is a chance for you to develop into the god you already are.

The question that needs to be asked is, "Why do you want to feel shame, guilt, or regret?" Does this seem like an odd inquiry? There are numerous reasons for this. For instance, there is something referred to as "secondary gain." This is the sort of thing which you probably won't be intentionally mindful of. It actually has some benefits for you, like getting more attention from others or being

freed from responsibilities. This could imply that you don't feel like you need to work as hard as you should. Therefore, because they provide you with an excuse not to have to commit yourself completely, your tricky mind will stop you from releasing your shame, guilt, or regret—of course, subconsciously.

We also hold onto shame, guilt, or regret because they have become habits. We do them automatically and unconsciously. We do not investigate those emotions. This is in part because these feelings are taught to us: If you hurt someone, you should feel bad about it or be ashamed of yourself. Why? As I mentioned, it is possible to acknowledge the action and move on. Someone may have been hurt by you. Okay, excuse yourself and move on. You might have done something wrong in the end. Move on after acknowledging it and learning from it.

Working with a trained psychologist or a professional counselor to process the shame and remove it from your life is highly recommended if you believe that shame (in particular) is driving your life because of something that was done to you, perhaps as a child.

A profound sense of unworthiness and inadequacy is one of the most significant internal wounds that the majority of us carry. This wound can be felt in many areas of our lives, including our creativity, sexuality, physical appearance, and sensitivity. However, the majority of the time, we experience it in a general sense that we are insufficient, that we are fundamentally flawed. The word for this wound is a shame.

Most of the time, we try to hide our shame by pretending to be okay and hiding it from ourselves and others. To persuade ourselves that we can "make it," we push, dress up, and fix ourselves. We may frequently turn around and succumb to insecurities and feelings of failure. Our lives become a constant struggle in either case. And when we look at the world through the prism of our shame, it appears to be a hostile environment in which we must fight and compete for survival or give up and resign.

The workshop will focus on both of these fundamental aspects of shame healing. The first is putting ourselves in the shoes of a wounded, shame-based child to fully comprehend and experience it. The second is acquiring the ability to take small risks to overcome the negative self-image that is brought on by shame and assist us in discovering our true selves.

If someone tries to make you feel guilty or doubtful, I would carefully examine the situation. If the situation occurred in the past, replay it over and over in your mind. This should gradually turn you into an observer who does not react, allowing you to begin comprehending all aspects of the situation. Consider the entire procedure and determine whether the individual is overly enthusiastic. Are they directing my efforts? Am I misinterpreting? Let go of your guilt and doubt if they are already present; they are premature, debilitating, and of no use to you at this time. Move your focus away from that or combine it with it, and then put in a lot of effort in the creation of new causes through new attitudes, ideas, and actions.

Only that good and bad karma are not determined by an individual is required. How would you become stable enough to handle the present and the future if you evaluated your past actions?

However, you did not intend to do what you did. Your heart should be cheered up by this alone. Sin can only be committed to doing wrong. You did not act in this manner.

If you're feeling down, you should go apologies to the person or people for this. The relationship that was erroneously disrupted can be repaired if you carry out this action with clarity and good intentions. By doing this, your souls will be freed from the karmic account.

When trying something new for the first time everyone develops a natural sense of right and wrong. You will never feel guilty if you listen to their inner voice. You should follow the advice of that inner voice to improve your life.

The spiritual abilities of the soul are also at their highest point in this body age. We are now able to comprehend and are prepared to choose our life's direction. Only a small number of people today follow the righteous path. That is a path that leads to the well-being of oneself and all others. because there are a lot of things that prevent you from doing the right thing. Ego, attachment, and selfishness are some of the most important ones.

Understanding karma's play is very difficult. Yet, life from a greater point of view is Perfect and loaded with valuable open doors. Gets another chance if any of them fail. Chances are endless. When you decide to give up, you are doomed to failure.

It is simple to choose between loving God and loving human souls. We have at least decided. First and foremost, one ought to have a love for God, the creator, followed by love for all souls—our brothers—and then for Nature—which provides us with life. Clear? Comprehend and deeply absorb this.

Love is not a one-time experience. Love is that feeling that should help you get bigger, better, and more powerful every day. It should not cause you to feel guilty. Freedom, accomplishments, giving, and sacrifice are all examples of love. All of these are expressions of true love.

True love is conscious of the soul. Our body is our tool for living this life.

We never die. The body is inert. Our connection to the supreme soul is eternal.

CHAPTER SIX

ACCEPTANCE

Poetry captures what life leaves out. We include in the film and the novel what we continue to lack in life.Because the first step has not yet been taken, love is completely absent.

The initial action is to esteem yourself for who you are; omit all obligations. Do not feel any responsibility in your heart! You are not to act differently; You are just to be who you are and not to do anything that doesn't belong to you. Relax! and just be who you are. Respect yourself for who you are. and be brave enough to sign your name. Stop copying other people's signatures.

It's not hard. Out of thinking, theories, and explanations comes consolation; Understanding is beyond acceptance. You console when you explain who you are. Acceptance comes when you understand. The need for consolation must be met; Acceptance is a natural process. Acceptance takes place; A good deed is a consolation.

"You are unhappy; Then you look for a theory to explain it: karmas from previous lives; you try to find a shelter somewhere. Or perhaps God is causing you pain so that you can mature: it is a test to develop - a comfort. Or it's just the way things are; When you philosophize, you assert that "I cannot be the exception because everyone is in misery." It is what it is: misery. There is no other option but to accept it. It must be accepted.' Then it's a comfort. After that, you put in a lot of effort to protect yourself.

The suffering is present. You investigate the misery, but you do not present any theory or explanation; You simply examine the reality of misery, and upon examination of the reality of misery, you discover a sudden acceptance. If someone inquires, "Why?" You won't be able to respond because you don't know why. You won't be able to demonstrate the reason. You will merely state, "It has occurred."

"All that is truly beautiful is always like love; acceptance is like love." When you fall in love with someone and they ask you, "Why?" Can you truly respond? Sometimes you try, but all of your responses are absurd. You say, "Because the woman is beautiful," but millions of people aren't in love with that woman. She would not have been available to you if she had been beautiful; instead, someone else would have grabbed her first. But no one else thinks she's beautiful, so you're doing the opposite.

You say, "I have fallen in love with her because she is beautiful." The reality is the exact opposite: Because you have fallen in love, she is stunning. The same woman will no longer appear beautiful to you when love ends one day; She might even begin to appear horrible and ugly. You can't even think about leaving her right now. You won't be able to bear her presence for even a moment when love vanishes one day.

It is effortless: It appears and departs. The same as love, acceptance is taking place. You don't look to the future or the past or the future to find an explanation when you are honest and in touch with the present reality; You simply investigate the situation.

Suffering is preferable to be consoled. It is preferable to be in pain rather than in consolation because, through pain, real acceptance can be achieved.

"There is no possibility through consolation; You've gone the wrong way. You never reach the truth through consolation; A dream has made you a victim. Because everything in the real will shatter your consolation, you will now have to live in your consolation and start to be afraid of reality. You won't look, you won't see directly, and you won't face the facts. If someone presents you with the facts, you will experience extreme restlessness, sweating, and nervousness because you will be aware that everything will now be shattered.

"Comfort is a conviction. There is no way a created thing has much value. Because it is your creation, it cannot be larger than you and will always be smaller than you. Acceptance happens because it is bigger than you.

The first step in absorbing any knowledge is to accept things as they are. It gives us the ability to intervene with wisdom and the gift of inner silence, a place where we can step back and make sense of the situation. When we no longer struggle with the questions "why," "how," and "how come" when we encounter people or situations, we can remain stable and upbeat and use our creativity to effectively deal with them because we no longer expend energy resisting them.

The act of wilfully moving in the direction where there is a way is what we mean when we talk about acceptance. It means to be able to tell the difference between things we can control and things we can't, focusing on the latter while ignoring the former. This does not imply that there is no desire for change; rather, it indicates that any desire for change is supported by a solution-oriented approach. The most effective strategy for making a difference is to first approach the current circumstance without judging it, accept it as it is, and then plant the seeds of change.

Our behavior on the outside is not the primary sign of tolerance; rather, how tolerant a person is is determined by what happens inside. For instance, can we say that we are tolerant if we do not respond when we are abused? We need to look inside ourselves to determine whether or not we are. Even if we keep our mouths shut, what if we are verbally abusing the other person without saying a word? What if we are thinking negative thoughts about the other person? Can we still be described as accommodating?

The response is no. This is since by not reacting immediately and thinking negative thoughts, we are only delaying our response. When that person comes back in front of us, these negative thoughts will build up inside of us, and if the situation is in our favor, they will all come out. Not only will the already-existing negativity explode, but it will also harm our minds and the relationships we have with one another. Therefore, true tolerance entails not being disturbed by any circumstance, words, or actions of others, and naturally reflecting the same behavior outside. Let's discover how to accomplish this.

For being steady from the inside, there is a pre-essential called the Force of Acknowledgment. We can tolerate more the more we accept. Tolerance does not imply forceful acceptance. Anything done with force is only temporary; once the force is removed, the situation or thought process returns to its previous state. So resistance must be long-lasting when it is finished based on acknowledgment.

The degree to which we accept the situation or the other person is primarily what determines our internal or physical response. External factors are only one part of the equation. There are numerous instances of this in our day-to-day lives. For instance, because we have already prepared ourselves to accept whatever is going to happen, if any adverse circumstance that was anticipated comes our way, we have a greater degree of tolerance for it.

When we work with others or interact with them, we frequently compare ourselves to other people. Acceptance increases in proportion to how similar they are to us and vice versa.

Therefore, we must first recognize and comprehend who we are as individuals. We are not the names, faces, skin tones, or religions we practice. We are souls—living energies that drive this body. We all have distinct identities, faces, and names.

There are no two people on this planet who share the same identity. Each of us was created uniquely by nature. It's a rule. Then, have we ever considered the reason we desire others to be like us? Why is this erroneous expectation outside of the norm? We are meant to be different, which is why we are different. However, the irony is that we cannot accept this difference.

In our original form, we are the representations of peace, love, purity, joy, bliss, knowledge, and power; each soul is the same way. The purpose of life is to experience all of these qualities, which we already possess. Today, we are all striving in the same direction to acquire these qualities.

Only when we are aware of who we are and what our true identity is can we comprehend and see others in their true identity. Only then can we appreciate that we are all working toward the same goal, which is to incorporate these qualities into our lives.

The path to unconditional acceptance for everyone and everything is this awareness. The longer we remain in this stage, which is referred to as the soul-conscious stage, When we keep our awareness of our soul and see others as souls, we will naturally begin to comprehend the actions of others and there will be no room for hurt feelings. This higher level of consciousness is the soil on which the blossoms of love and acceptance thrive. As a result, this love and acceptance are free from expectation, impartial, and universal.

Since we are all a part of a wonderful drama with different roles and the same goals, we can appreciate each person's role and ignore our differences. The power of tolerance will be increased as a result of our instillation of unrestricted acceptance of everyone and everything.

As previously stated, practicing soul-consciousness is a means of tolerance and acceptance. Being aware that we are souls and that other people are also souls is the fundamental definition of the soul-conscious stage. But is awareness sufficient? Even though awareness is the first step toward becoming soul-conscious, practicing it is more important. Being soul conscious entails consistently putting one's original soul qualities into practice.

A soul-conscious person is filled with peace, love, purity, happiness, etc., in every thought, word, and action. However, to maintain these qualities even in challenging circumstances, we must incorporate them into our daily lives.

Don't be critical of what happens to you. Instead, believe that better things will always come your way and that everything happens for a reason. True acceptance begins at that point.

CHAPTER SEVEN

REALIZATION

There are numerous inquiries. The initial: Is self-actualization a fundamental human need?

Try to comprehend what self-actualization entails first.

Man is potential from birth. He is only a possibility, not a real person. Man is only a possibility when he is born, not a reality. He might turn into something; he might achieve the realization of his probability, or he may not accomplish it.

The opportunity could be utilized or not. Additionally, nature does not compel you to become real. You're free. You have the option of becoming real; You can decide not to take any action. Man is created from a seed. As a result, no man is born satisfied—merely with the possibility of satisfying himself.

Self-actualization becomes a fundamental need if that is the case, which it is. You'll feel like you're missing something if you don't become what you can or were meant to be if your destiny isn't fulfilled if you don't achieve and if your seed doesn't become a tree that is fulfilled. Additionally, everyone has the impression that he lacks something. The fact that you are not yet real is the real cause of your sense of missing out.

You are not lacking in wealth, position, prestige, or power. Even if you get everything you want, be it wealth, power, prestige, or anything else, you will always feel like something is missing from you because it has nothing to do with anything outside of you. It has to do with your personal development. This sense of something missing will be felt unless you experience fulfillment, a flowering, or an inner satisfaction in which you feel that "Now this is what I was meant to be." Furthermore, you can't replace this sense of something missing with anything else.

The fundamental need is actualizing oneself. And by "basic," I mean that you won't feel fulfilled if your needs are met, including self-realization and self-actualization. Even if you achieve self-actualization and nothing else fulfills you, you will still experience deep and complete fulfillment. In search of fulfillment, you continue to pursue various desires. Because one desire leads to another, that search never ends. One desire leads to ten. You will never reach a state of bliss where there are no desires if you pursue them.

However, if you try something else—methods of self-actualization, methods of realizing your inner potentiality, methods of making them actual—you'll find that the more you become actual, the less you'll feel desires because, in reality, you only feel them when you're empty inside. Desire ceases when you are not empty inside.

How should self-actualization be handled? Two concepts must be comprehended. Self-actualization does not imply that you will be self-actualized if you become a great poet, musician, or painter. Naturally, a portion of you will be realized, and even that brings a great deal of contentment.

A portion of you will be fulfilled, but not the entirety if you fulfill your potential to be a good musician and become a musician. You won't be able to express your remaining humanity. You'll be unfair. The remaining portion will have remained as a stone dangling from your neck while one portion will have expanded.

What makes a man complete? What does it mean to be a complete man? First, it means to be centered; exist only with a center.

You are something right now, and then something else. I typically ask people who come to see me, "Where do you feel your center — in the heart, in the mind, in the navel, where?" In the center of sex? Where? Where are you most at ease? "Sometimes I feel it in the head, sometimes in the heart, and sometimes I do not feel it at all" is a common statement. So I tell them to close their eyes in front of me right now and feel it. The majority of the time, this occurs: "Just now, for a moment, I feel that I am centered in the head," they proclaim. However, the following instant, they are absent. "I am in the heart," they declare. And when the center regains its position, it is either at the sex center or somewhere else.

You aren't centered; You only briefly center yourself. You continue to shift because every moment has its center. When the mind is working, the head feels like the center. You can feel it in your heart when you are in love. You are in a state of confusion when you are not specifically engaged in any activity because you are unable to locate the center. After all, you can only do so while working on something. The center of the body then shifts to a specific area. However, YOU are not focused. You won't be able to locate your center of being if you don't do anything.

A man who doesn't keep his center will always go to extremes. He will eat a lot, overeat, or fast when he eats, but he cannot eat healthily. It's easy to fast, and it's fine to overeat. He can be involved, committed, or in the world, or he can leave it, but he will never be balanced. He will never be able to stay in the middle because you cannot understand what the middle is if you are not centered. The person who is centered is always in the middle of everything and never at the other end of the spectrum. According to Buddha, his eating is healthy; Neither fasting nor overeating is involved. His work is correct—never too much or too little. He is always balanced, no matter who he is.

How can we put the Self-Realization hypothesis to the test? Our findings must be repeatable to be considered valid, right?

Self-Realization is a process that is repeatable and has specific effects on various aspects of our being, whether physical, mental, emotional, or spiritual if the experience and verifiable proof of its outcomes can all be obtained consistently in nearly all humans. Understanding and experiencing the components of the subtler self in a clear, unambiguous, and consistent manner is made possible by awakening the subtle energy.

Can someone provide you with evidence of the Self-Realization process to bolster your belief in its existence?

That would seldom happen. Humans tend to demand proof first, which may explain why only a small percentage of people ever achieve Self-Realization. However, the issue is that self-realization is an individual, internal process experienced by each person; As a result, external data, instruments, and measurements make it difficult to "prove." All of the evidence you need is provided by the experience itself.

Perhaps this intelligent capsule was constructed in this manner by the universal power of creation to eliminate those who were not yet prepared for it! And if they weren't, they missed out on this experience because they either didn't look for it in the first place, they looked for the journey but didn't try Self-Realization as a hypothesis, or they didn't have the patience to keep looking until they felt the subtler self's effect on their central nervous system.

Yes, there are a few points along the way where people can get lost! There is a further possibility: if the well-intentioned are tempted away from their spiritual journey and their subtler selves by the pull of the material self. Sadly, this is quite common. The ego exists because we keep pushing desire, keep trying to get something and keep getting ahead of ourselves. That is the very thing that the ego does—it jumps ahead of itself, into the future, and tomorrow. The ego is created by the leap into the non-existent. It is like a mirage because it emerges from the non-existent. There is no other substance in it but desire. There is no other component to it other than thirst. It only encompasses the future and nothing else.

The future belongs to the ego, not the present. The ego appears to be quite substantial if you are in the future. On the off chance that you are in the present, the self-image is an illusion, it begins vanishing.

Desire can't be stopped; It can only be understood. The stopping is in our very understanding. Keep in mind that there is no way to stop wanting, and real life can only occur when desire stops.

Understanding the desire is essential. It's understandable to you. You can see how pointless it is. It is necessary to have a direct perception and an immediate penetration. If you just look at the desire for what it is, you will discover that it is false and non-existent. And both your desire and something else within you drop simultaneously.

The ego and desire work together, they work together. Desire can't exist without the ego, and the ego can't exist without the desire. Ego is introjected desire, while desire is projected ego. Together, they are two aspects of the same phenomenon.

You can't decrease the distance between you and your expectation. Horizon is hope. You attempt to connect with the horizon, with hope, and with a desire

that is projected. Because the horizon does not exist, you cannot build a bridge toward it; instead, you can only dream about the bridge. The desire is a bridge, a dream bridge. You and the non-existent cannot be joined.

The only thing you can hope for is your hopelessness, the only thing you can desire is your hopelessness, and the entirety of existence suddenly begins to assist you in your tremendous helplessness.

It is standing by. It does not intervene when it observes that you are working independently. It lingers. Because it is not in a hurry, it can sit there forever. It's been a long time.

The entirety of existence rushes toward you and enters you the moment you are not alone, the moment you fall, and the moment you disappear. And for the first time, activities begin.

You make your fantasy around you and if you become conscious you will keep on dreaming. Because the world you know is the world of your dreams, the world is not real. At the point when dreams drop and you just experience the world that is there, then, at that point, this present reality. However, whatever you see right now is a projected lie and not the truth. That is what a mirage means. And if you can see, even for a brief moment, and if you are willing to let yourself see, you will find immense blessings everywhere—in the clouds, in the sun, and on Earth.

The world is beautiful. However, I'm not referring to your world; rather, I'm referring to mine. Your world is a projected world, and it is very unpleasant because it was created by you. You are projecting your ideas onto the real world by using them as a screen.

When I say that the world is real, that it is incredibly beautiful, that it is luminous with infinity, that it is light and delight, and that it is a celebration, I mean that the world is real. If you give up your dreams, I'm referring to my world or yours.

Regardless of whether a portion of the person's mind, ego, or body passed away at any given time, the person remained. It was renovated numerous times, decorated numerous times, and slightly altered on occasion, but the continuity remained.

CHAPTER EIGHT

DISTANCE IS NECESSARY

It is essential to recognize that you are not the mind—neither the bright nor the dark one. It is impossible to separate yourself from your ugly side if you identify with your beautiful side; Both of them are facets of the same thing. You can keep it as-is or dispose of it in its entirety, but you cannot divide it.

Additionally, the desire to select the attractive and bright is the root of all human anxiety; He wants to pick all the good things and leave the bad things behind. However, he is unaware that there can be no silver linings without a dark cloud. The background, or dark cloud, is absolutely necessary for the positive aspects to emerge.

Anxiety is choosing.

Choosing is causing you problems.

Having no choice means: There is the mind, and it has both a good side and a bad side. So what? How does it relate to you? Why are you concerned about it?

When you are unable to choose, all worries vanish. There is a profound acceptance that this is the way the mind must be and is its nature and that it is not your problem because you are not the mind. There would have been no issue if you were the mind. Then who would make the decision and consider transcending? And who would attempt to comprehend and accept acceptance?

You are isolated, absolutely discrete.

You are nothing more than a witness.

But you're just being an observer who becomes attached to anything he likes and forgets that the bad is just behind it as a shadow. The good side doesn't bother you; in fact, you look forward to it. The problem arises when the opposite side asserts, at which point you become divided.

However, you initiated the entire issue. You changed from being merely a witness to an individual. The biblical account of the fall is nothing more than fiction. However, this is the real fall—from being a witness to becoming associated with something and losing your witnessing—and it is the fall.

Give it a shot once in a while: Allow the mind to be as it pleases. Be aware that you are not it. Additionally, you are in for a major surprise. Because its power comes from your identification, the mind begins to lose power as you become less identified; It draws blood from you. The mind, on the other hand, begins to contract when you distance yourself.

The revelation comes on the day when you are completely disconnected from the mind, even for a brief moment: the mind simply goes away; It no longer exists. It suddenly vanishes from places where it was so full and continuous—day in and day out, waking and sleeping. When you look around, all you see is nothingness and emptiness.

The goose that is not in the mind's bottle is awareness. However, you are insisting that it is inside and requesting assistance from all parties. Additionally, there are idiots who will assist you with escape strategies. Because they have no idea what's going on, I call them fools.

Since the goose is out and has never entered, the issue of releasing it does not arise.

The mind is nothing more than a stream of thoughts that appear on the brain's screen in front of you. You are a spectator. However, once you begin to associate beautiful things with you, those are bribes. Because the mind cannot exist without duality, once you get caught up in the beautiful things, you also get caught up in the ugly things.

Both the mind and awareness cannot exist in the absence of duality.

Both the mind and awareness are dual.

Simply watch. You won't learn any solutions from me. I demonstrate the solution:

Simply return a little and observe.

Put some distance between yourself and your thoughts.

Compulsions are choices made in ignorance, but everyone makes choices. Let's say right now you're angry. Actually, you have chosen to be angry. You believe that is the best course of action, but the decision is made so consciously that it becomes a compulsion. On a different level, it is happening compulsively. Therefore, you are living by choice, but you are making choices without realizing it—unconscious choices. The goal is to change into a more conscious decision-maker.

Even when you do something as simple as get up in the morning, your unconscious decision is to not get up. Pull the sheet slightly higher up over your face as the sun rises. This is an unintentional decision. Your body wants to stay in the bed for a while longer. It refuses to stand for numerous reasons. In many ways, you are not looking forward to the day because there are so many aspects of life and so many limitations in your experience.

There are many levels of awareness. All that is available to you is what you are aware of. This must be comprehended. You are sitting here right now, and you are unaware that a massive dinosaur is standing behind you. Don't look back to see. Is it available to you? No. It matters not that such a massive animal is standing there because you are unaware of it and do not recognize it as such. You are limited to what you are aware of. Your awareness is currently limited to a small portion of your life. The whole idea of spirituality is to become aware of everything you are, so before you go, you know life and experience it in all of its aspects. Spirituality is the ability to live fully. You can't just know a small part of your life to know life in all its dimensions. You need to know everything.

So, how do you know if you want to know everything? If we must use an analogy, let's say we reduce the lighting voltage. Let's say there is only one light. It only lights up a certain amount, and we only see that much. You can suddenly see a lot more if you raise the voltage because the light has spread. Like this, awareness is the same. Everything in your body, mind, and energy is operating at a certain limited voltage right now. When you turn up the voltage, you suddenly start seeing a lot of things you had never seen before.

To put it simply and technically, you need to raise your voltage in some way. You can simply increase your voltage through enthusiasm, but that will not take you far. Other kinds of technologies can constantly raise your voltage in a certain way.

While life outside of you is completely under your control, it should happen inside like a huge explosion. When you enter a phase like this, you will notice that even the outside tends to happen like an explosion for a while, but you will eventually gain some control over it. There is control outside, but there is an explosion inside. That ought to be the case. Your life should be an absolute explosion every moment of it. It is properly controlled outside of your control. You will be able to use your physical body, your mind, and your emotions to the fullest when it is like this. Because your voltage is full, you suddenly start doing things you never thought you could.

When you are constantly generating many conceptions, such as thinking about good and bad and the like, the first introduction to the view of naturally arisen innermost awareness cannot be made.

Therefore, leave whatever appears to your mind among the various phenomena of the world—people, buildings, mountains, your work, your friends, your problems, and the like—as just an appearance without making any adjustments to your mind, such as conceptually working at analysis. Don't get involved and polluted with identifying it and thinking, "This is such-and-such."

Inner awareness that has arisen naturally exists within you; It is present naturally and was not created or constructed by superficial circumstances.

Instead, it is original wisdom, flowing awareness whose continuum is fundamental and uncreated in and of itself. Don't let new ideas that are only superficially fabricated emerge, as you now see. Don't come up with new ideas, and even if you do notice that ideas have been created, don't force yourself to believe that they should be withdrawn; simply allow them to vanish.

You will not be influenced by conventional ideas if you can make all of these phenomena appear as the vibration of your deepest awareness without departing from that mind's domain. You are enlightened even when you are acting in the world when you directly identify your fundamental entity and continuously and forever determine its meaning in meditative equilibrium.

CHAPTER NINE

MOVE ON BITCH!

We have options when we use the word "choice"; there are options available for everything. However, there is a fascinating aspect to it. The mind actually decides between options "A" and "B." No matter what it has decided, whether "A" or "B," it is unilateral and never complete.

There is no choice when one lives fully. However, the human mind operates in extremes as a result of this choice. Because we have choices—either I will have this or I will have that—we all experience extremes. The mind never finds a happy medium.

Our sages have always advised us to live in the middle, never the extremes, according to the scriptures. In this regard, their message has always been very clear: stop choosing, stop clinging to choices, and just let life and the beautiful, blissful moments be.

Choices, polarities, and eventually the mind all need to go to see the beauty of life and live it. Because the mind sometimes tends to cling to pain, negative experiences, and even thoughts in the form of memories, one must learn to be in a let-go state. However, for us to be in a state of let-go, we must always be aware of how our mind works and its natural tendency to choose between two extremes in every situation.

The let-go state will eventually occur if the mind is constantly observed for this tendency. In this state of let-go, pleasure, and bliss can only be experienced.

The deepest sense of respect for existence as it is in the state of letting go. For instance, the flower cannot blossom unless the dew drops fall from it. The key to the flowers' blossoming and success is to let go. Additionally, the flowers, unable to release the dew drops, wither and remain lifeless.

The possibility of flowering after the dew drops have vanished is shown in three scenarios in this painting. a flower that has the potential to blossom but will not be able to do so until it lets go of the dew drops that are in it; thirdly, the gray flowers that cling to the dew droplets wither and do not bloom.

The majority of us live lives filled with desperation, suffering, and agony because we are too afraid to let go of the everyday things in our lives. Let-go is

more than just feeling like you have no choice; It is the transformation of life into a state of absolute bliss and joy.

Strange is the law of inner victory. If you want to win in the outside world, you have to be violent, aggressive, and willing to fight. The internal world is exactly the opposite: If you want to win, you can't fight; you can't even think about fighting. You must be loving, nonviolent, and compassionate rather than violent. Simply put, the only way to succeed on the inner journey is to be able to surrender. A complete let-go, surrender, is necessary for victory.

There is some truth to the fear; You may revert to your previous routines. However, don't be afraid; just keep an eye out; In the meantime, if that occurs, Falling into old routines does not necessarily mean that it will occur to everyone. It will only occur to friends who have imposed the new discipline on themselves that if they let go, they will revert to their previous selves.

However, it will be beneficial because it will demonstrate that you have not become what you thought you had become. It was merely a controlled, suppressed, and inhibited phenomenon that was enforced. It will become clear to you if you let go.

Therefore, it will benefit both types of people. By letting go, those who have matured into a new way of life will ascend. Those who have forced themselves into the new way of life and have had some resistance, a part of them fighting against it, will lose control if they let go. That's also positive. You will realize that you are not who you thought you were.

Don't try to suppress the old pattern right now. Instead, watch it. It must be let go, not suppressed. Discipline is used in repression while witnessing is used in dropping. Witness the previous pattern.

Avoid becoming associated with it.

And as you move away from the new way of life that you forced yourself into, if you continue to watch and let go, even when you see the old pattern start to emerge, that too will disappear because it is also something that society forces you into. The same cannot be natural. And only when everything forced has vanished are you your true self.

To me, being spiritual is natural. Something absurd has been taught by all religions: Spirituality opposes naturalism. Therefore, everyone has suppressed the natural self and acted like a spiritual self, even though he is not one. Every one of the religions together has plotted against humankind to make scoundrels.

My goal is to make a man who is human, free of guilt, and willing to accept all of his flaws and failures. The seed of your transformation lies in this complete acceptance of who you are as a natural being. Additionally, it is growth when it occurs on its own. It is not a growth when you force it to, but rather merely a mask. And if you wear a mask, you can fool yourself even in front of a mirror: You might begin to believe that this is your face. Letting go means that your ego, personality, and masks will all fall off as well.

Continue doing so until all of these things vanish and you discover a pure naturalness, a spontaneity of being. Therefore, you shouldn't be afraid. The majority of you will discover that whatever you have continues to grow. Some of you will discover that you have only managed a small amount of progress; You've been playing it safe. Then you'll fall back into your old routine.

Avoid repeating the same error this time around. Keep an eye on things and keep going through the same letting-go process. Your previous habits are also false; They too will vanish. You will return to your natural self, to your authentic self, if the let-go is complete. That, in my opinion, marks the beginning of your enlightenment and self-realization. However, you must first discover your natural source before it can begin. They cannot become enlightened: your masks, patterns of hypocrisy, and pretended selves. Enlightenment can only come from the face you always knew. Therefore, the most important thing for a traveler on the path is to be original and natural.

When things are uncertain, it's hard to relax. Any fear of death will vanish if you are aware that you will die today. What good is it to waste time? Only one day remains for you: live as fully as possible, with as much intensity as possible.

"Death might not occur. People who live their lives completely and intensely are immune to death. And even if it comes, those who have lived their entire lives will gladly accept it because it will be a great relief. Because they lived so completely and intensely, they are sick of living, and death comes to them like a friend. Death follows life in the same way that the night is a wonderful time of relaxation after a long day's work. There is nothing horrible about death; There is nothing cleaner out there...

“If there is a fear of death, it indicates that there are a few gaps that cannot be filled by living. Therefore, these fears of death are very helpful and indicative. They show you that you need to move a little faster in your dance and that you need to share the torch of your life.

"Dance so quickly that the dancer vanishes and all that is left is the dance.

"Then you cannot be visited by any fear of death.

"And the anxiety of having to leave all of this beauty, love, and friendship."

“Who cares about tomorrow if you are completely here now?

Tomorrow will deal with itself. Who is requesting tomorrow from you?

Even today is sufficient on its own. Additionally, you must realize that each moment has a conclusion.

CHAPTER TEN

CONCLUSIONS; LET'S FLY HIGH

1. Every person in the world has some kind of weakness.

Do you know someone who seems to have everything?

We live, considering that one weakness as the center of life. Because of this, there is always sorrow and dissatisfaction in our minds. Weakness is acquired by man by birth or by association. But our mind makes that weakness it's limit. But some people defeat that weakness with hard work. What is the difference between them and other people? Have you ever thought about it?

The answer to this is very simple, the person who is not defeated by weakness or the person who dares to work hard, becomes free from the trap of weakness. Weakness may be given by God, but it is the dignity that builds a man's mind.

2. The struggle is another name for the future. When the desire that arises in the heart is not fulfilled, then the heart plans for the future. Keeps imagining that the wish will be fulfilled in the future.

But life is neither in the future nor in the past. Life is the name of this moment in which we are living now. That means the experience of this moment is the experience of life. But even after knowing all this, we do not understand such a small truth. Either we sit surrounded by the memories of the past, or we keep making plans for the future.

And life passes amid these absurd thoughts.

If we keep one truth in our mind that neither we can see the future nor we can create the future, we can only embrace the world with patience and courage, then isn't every moment of life full of happiness? Will it be filled?

3. We all know that the attainment of knowledge always comes with dedication. But what is the real significance of surrender?

Man's mind always creates various obstacles in the attainment of knowledge. Sometimes one gets jealous of another student, sometimes doubts arise about the lessons taught, and sometimes the punishment given by the Guru fills the mind with ego. Say? Doesn't it happen?

Don't know how useless thoughts distract the mind and due to this confused state of mind, we are not able to get knowledge. A worthy state of mind is created only by surrender. Surrender destroys the ego of man. There is no limit to knowledge and neither to the wise in this world.

Knowledge may be of anything, but to get it, our dedication to the Guru is more important than the Guru!

4. There comes a time in the life of every human being when all dreams and all the hopes are shattered. All the events of life get scattered. There is religion on one side and happiness on the other side, this is called the crisis of religion. When the attainment of religion takes the form of trouble and the renunciation of religion becomes happiness. Most people do not understand this illusion, and we do not experience any kind of struggle. We are easily drawn toward happiness like a fly is attracted to Jagger. In fact, times of religious crisis take us closer to our destination. If we are not afraid of struggles and are not attracted to happiness, then the peace of mind is not far away!

5. When two people come close, they try to create limits and boundaries for each other. If we consider all the relationships, we will be able to see that the basis of all these relationships is the boundaries that we create for others. And if someone unknowingly breaks these limits, then at that very moment our heart gets filled with anger.

What is the actual form of these limitations? Have we ever thought?

By boundaries, we do not allow another person to decide, we impose our decision on that person. It means to say that we reject someone's freedom. And when freedom is denied, his heart fills with sadness and when he breaks boundaries, our heart fills with anger.

But if each other's freedom is respected, then there is no need for any limits or boundaries.

6. Such an incident comes into everyone's life when there is a determination in the heart, to tell the truth, but the truth does not come out of the mouth. Some fear surrounds the mind. Talking about an incident or event or forgetting to speak about it, is it true?

No! These are just facts! That is, it is a normal thing to speak only as it happened, but sometimes there is fear even while speaking about that fact. Perhaps the thought of someone else's feelings comes in the mind. The fear that others will be hurt also stops words.

Then what is this truth? Have we ever thought?

When someone speaks facts despite being in fear, then it is called truth. Truth is nothing but fearlessness and there is no time to be fearless because fearlessness is the nature of the soul. That is, isn't every moment a moment to tell the truth?

7. Based on past impressions, we imagine future happiness and sorrow. We plan today to remove the cause of future unhappiness. But by eradicating the coming crisis today, do we get benefit or harm?

We never ask this question.

The truth is that crisis and its solution are born together, for the individual as well as for the world. If you look at your past or history, you will find that whenever there is a crisis, the power to solve it also takes birth. This is the trend of the world. In reality, the crisis is the reason for the birth of Shakti. When a person comes out of a crisis, then one step further increases. He shines more. He is full of confidence, not only for himself but also for the world. The birth of a crisis is the birth of an opportunity. Opportunity to change yourself. An opportunity to elevate yourself. Opportunity to make yourself strong and knowledgeable.

The one who can do this does not face any problems, but the one who cannot do this, himself is a problem for the world.

8. Sometimes some incident breaks all the plans of a man's life and the man considers that trauma as the center of his life. But, Is the future built based on man's plans?

No! Just as the first person to climb a high mountain makes a plan sitting at the bottom of that mountain, does the same plan take that man to the top of the mountain?

No! As he climbs up, he has to face new challenges and new crises. He makes his own decision on each post. He has to change his plans for each post.

Furthermore, he cannot make the mountain worthy of himself, he only makes himself worthy of the mountain.

Is it the same with life?

When a man considers the traumas of his life as his center, then he can never become successful, nor can he attain happiness and peace. That's why don't make life worthy of you but make yourself worthy of life, that is the only way to success and happiness.

9. Every moment of life is a moment of decision. The decision has to be taken on every path regarding some other post, and the decision leaves its impact. Decisions made today create happiness and unhappiness in the future, not only for ourselves but also for our families and generations to come. When a dilemma comes to the front, the mind becomes restless and filled with uncertainty. That moment of decision becomes a war and the mind becomes the battlefield!

Most of the decisions we take are not to solve the dilemma, but only to calm the mind.

Will the war-torn mind be able to take a worthy decision?

When someone decides with a calm mind, he creates a happy future for himself, but when someone decides to calm his mind, that person plants a tree full of thorns for himself in the future!

10. When a man does not consider himself worthy of the upcoming struggles in life, then he abandons the virtues and adopts the bad qualities. Weakness takes birth in the mind of a man only when he does not have confidence in his mind. Self-confidence holds goodness.

Is this confidence?

When a man believes that the struggle of life makes him weak, then he does not have faith in himself. Instead of going beyond the struggle, he starts looking for ways to get rid of the struggle. But when he understands that this struggle will make him more powerful, then his enthusiasm increases with each struggle. That means confidence is nothing but a state of mind. It is just a point of view to see life. And the outlook of life is in the control of man himself.

We have always heard that if you want to move forward in life, always support your loved ones.

This thing is true. We must support our loved ones, but before supporting them, we need to know who are our own. Are ours the ones with whom we have blood relations?

Ours are the ones who inspire us to show hospitality, to move forward, and to support us. And those whose support leads to the destruction of society or loss of religion, are not our relatives even though they are our relatives. That's why, when you choose to make someone your own, consider them as your own who support you and not those who take us on the path of ignorance.

11. We always want to be close to those whom we love. We do not want him or her to be away from us ever. But after a time, being away from loved ones is necessary for progress.

If you keep guiding your child or your close ones at every turn of their life, how will your child learn to choose his path? How will He or She learn to fight the thorns that come his or her way?

That's why after a time, the distance created from your loved ones is always beneficial.

CHAPTER ELEVEN

SITUATIONSHIP (BONUS CHAPTER)

Many years ago, I had heard somewhere that if any woman is with you in any form in your life, then understand that the form of God himself is walking with you.

Well, this thing proved to be true for me in many situations and painful in some situations. But there was never any regret of that pain in my mind. In my opinion, there should be no regret for beautiful pains.

In the case of girls, my luck has always been crooked.

Well, if I start all these things then maybe the night will pass.

There were also meetings. There was love too. There was also a dispute. And perhaps the controversy has given me the ability to live further.

But what would happen then that you had dreamed of getting such a girl whom you were always dousing for since childhood, and you get her?

How beautiful those times would have been. When all your search ends on one person. How beautiful that moment would have been.

I have come face to face with such times last month.

So college days were going on. It was the last semester. Only 5 months were left before the college ended.

For a long time, I used to notice a girl. Short hair, beautiful eyes, charming style, fragrant voice.

It seemed as if time had stopped. She used to sit alone on the last seat in the class engrossed in her world. And I was always surrounded by my friends. But no matter what, my eyes used to go toward her, and then I did not feel like taking my eyes off her. The process of meeting through eyes went on for about 8 months.

When I used to come back home from college exhausted, her picture used to keep roaming somewhere in my mind. Well, time went on. December had arrived and along with it came college exams. Everyone on my side got busy preparing for the exams.

The date was **7 December.**

I was coming out in a dirty mood after finishing my exam. So my eyes fell on the oldest tree planted in the college. The same girl was sitting below who had given me sleepless nights. Our eyes met and we both just kept looking at each other. Time had stopped. There were gusts of cold wind. The shower of peace had started raining. The whole pain of spoiling the exam was over. "Ishq" was dancing like a prankster.

Then suddenly a voice comes from behind – "The children whose exams are over should go to their homes."

That voice was of the watchman of the college.

If I was the principal of the college, I would have fired him from the job on the same day.

Well, it was written in my destiny to meet only the sight, so what could I do? Then I started walking towards my house.

The same day in the evening when I was drinking coffee, then a notification comes to my phone. As soon as I saw that notification, I went mad with

happiness. I was like flying in the air. The silence of happiness was scattered all around.

That message was from the same girl. It was a matter of appreciating luck because the girl about whom I was thinking till just 2 minutes ago, suddenly got a message like this for the first time.

Before moving forward in the story, let me tell you that I am very fond of writing and poems. And these two qualities of mine were very similar to that girl. For the last 8 months, we used to just like each other's stories. This was our way of talking. When she used to enjoy my poems, she used to congratulate me by sending emojis and I used to do the same process. But we never talked.

Another interesting thing is that almost all our qualities and habits are similar. And this was the biggest reason for liking her. Whatever I wished to get in a girl, I used to see all those wishes in this girl.

December 3, 00:17 AM

A post shared by her stated:

" People romanticize reading poems like silently drinking hot tea, sitting under a blanket by the fireplace like in a period drama, etc."

After this message from her, I had got an excuse to continue talking to her. Now there was no question of retreat.

I replied: Pal, I don't know whether it's a form of precognition or anything else but I just had your glimpse in my head 2 minutes ago, and here is your text. Haha!

She: Haha! WOW! I've superpowers.

Me: No! I've Manifested powers. Haha!

She:- For how many days do we have to manifest so that the person in front should reply?

Me:- It is not right to reveal this secret!

She:- Many of our habits match. Do you know?

Me:- It gives me relief to see that someone like me who knows how to move with peace and beauty and who understands that beauty of life has no limitations, who know joy and happiness in life usually depends on contemplating people and thing around us!

She:- Yes, I believe that people need to understand the value of small things and how little words can create a huge impact. I also believe that they should stop trying to appear cool and instead begin to show more concern for their surroundings.

Me:- Also you know how to be beautifully expressive without wasting words.

December 3, 10:19 PM

A post was shared by me stated, " Thinking about the countless times art and music and cinema and literature have saved and comforted me during difficult times I owe my happiness to everyone dedicated to their craft"

She replied;

Everyone needs art, music, and literature to feel something and survive this brutal world. Poets convert their sadness into wonderful words. I feel blue every time.

December 4, 10:47 AM

She:- Hello there!

Me:- Hello!

She:- Have you checked out this amazing poet from Pakistan? He writes so well. You should listen to him.

Me:- I already did! He's in my top playlist.

She got jealous. But that jealousy was filled with love. Whether it is a coincidence or fate, whatever things she used to send me, I had either heard or seen them before. I used to get a chance to tease her.

December 14, 10:45 AM

Location:- College

I was chatting with my friends in the college garden when I saw her. We both saw each other. She also took the initiative to come towards me but I stole my eyes. At that very moment, I regretted that I should not have done this. She felt very bad about this. Well, we both went on our way.

I was sitting at home in the evening, thinking that she must not have liked it today. There was no message from her that day. My heart was filled with uneasiness. Somehow I mustered up the courage and messaged her.

Me:- Hey! How are you?

She:- Fine!

Me:- You don't seem fine. Tell me, what's the matter?

She:- Do you want to know?

Me:- Of course, everything should be transparent.

She:- My intentions are not to hurt you but I have been noticing that you always pretended not to see me even when I was there in front of you. I really don't know why you do this to me. I suspect it has something to do with your introverted character but you make me feel invisible and it hurts me!

This thing of hers was going to make my heart sad. She was right. It was all my fault and I regret it too.

I replied;

I was sure this would be the reason. But it is not like that. I admit that I am very clumsy in the first few meetings.

Not a single moment has passed when I have not noticed you. Just that little shame comes in between. But I am working on that. I promise, next time you will not get any chance to complain. But these small mistakes do not mean that you get angry or stop talking. Never do this in the future. If anything of mine hurts you, then you interrupt me at the same time.

She:- It's okay yaar! Relax. I'm there!

Everything started running again as before. We were getting closer. The process of getting to know each other had already begun. Our talks were full of beauty and humor, which was bringing us closer.

December 24, 9:30 PM

She:- Hey! It's Christmas tomorrow. Let's meet.

Me:- Yeah sure! Where?

She:- Pick me up from Chirag Delhi metro station at 2 PM tomorrow. I'll be waiting for you.

You decide the place but make sure it's crowd free. I want nature in silence where we can explore each other and have a great evening.

Me:- Done! I'll be there at 2 PM sharp. Can't wait to see you.

The next day was Christmas. On that day there are inevitably a lot of crowds everywhere. But even then I searched for a peaceful place. Now just waiting for morning.

I got ready well and reached the place called by her at exactly 2 o'clock. Now just waiting for her arrival. Suddenly a dreamy fragrance wafted near me. When I turned back, she was in front of me.

> *"In every gooey rom-com, the moment when two people first meet, they often find themselves falling in love. With a slow-motion shot and an inspirational song playing in the background, two perfect strangers instantly become one hot and heavy couple. Of course, no matter how many romantic movies you've watched, or how many times you've been in love yourself, it's natural to wonder, what does love at first sight feel like?*
>
> *Whether all your fears seem to slip away or you feel calm and confident when you started talking to them, love at first sight can mean something different to everyone. Though an instant spark sounds like the height of romance, love follows its timeline. Sometimes, you know you're in love the second you lock your eyes, and other times, you don't know you're in love until months or even years later. Whatever the case, relationships unfold in their own time."*

We hugged."

The cab was waiting for us to drop us at my chosen destination.

It would probably be difficult for me to describe our first meeting. Because we talked with eyes and not with words. When I saw the eyes, I kept looking. Eyes like Ghazals. Eyes in which the sky and the earth are imprisoned. Such eyes that if raised, become a flood and if bowed down, become blessings.

A meeting that cannot be described in words.

Well, time passed. Things got deeper. The meetings started happening more and more. Time was passing and along with it, my restlessness was also increasing. Now I did not like being away from her even for a moment. I agree that there was not much time between us that both of us could come into a relationship. But the nature of us humans is such that we do not listen to anyone other than our heart in matters of love.

As the days of the end of college were getting closer, the fear of losing her was sitting inside me.

According to me, it should not take much time to express love, no matter what the result may be. If the thing is being said with a true heart, then it should be acceptable.

The restlessness was touching its peak. There was a strange commotion in the heart.

Then one day I gathered all my courage and decided to express my love.

February 9, 11:03 PM

I texted;

Listen!

I am not able to survive peacefully now. I am starting to lose my patience. Whatever I am about to say, you may consider it as anything, but for me, it is my love. This is my truth. And I am saying all this very thoughtfully.

I can't stop thinking about you. I have started liking you a lot. I see my shadow in you.

The person I always wanted, all those qualities are within you.

I am in a lot of pain and I cannot bear it anymore.

I have started loving you a lot.

It doesn't matter to me how much time has passed since we met. I just know that whatever I am saying, I am saying it with full sincerity and heart. I have done it with full devotion.

If we remain just friends then our bond may never be fulfilled. And I feel it with all my heart.

I am willing to give you all that you'll be needed in upcoming times.

I'm saying this practically and You can try me on this.

The day you will feel that you made a mistake by coming with me, then you can confess it in front of me, then I will go away from you forever.

I am sending my feelings in a letter to you. If possible, you should reply to the letter with the letter itself.

"*The Letter*

That you "hit the ground talking!" Non-stop, with total understanding! The whole time you are together. I find you attractive. Not necessarily in a sexual way, though that's often there if the combination is right. The exposure is always brief. As if you meet on a train platform, committed to trains going in opposite directions.

The phenomenon is ALWAYS instantly mutual. As you will learn when they eagerly agree to your evaluation. I know No connection, but still, you seem so personal!

You walk in charisma, like the night of cloudless climes and starry skies; and all that's best of dark and bright.

Since there's no help
Will you come and let us part?
Shake hands forever, cancel all society vows?
Last gasp of love's latest breath?
When my pulse fails, passion speechless lies?
When faith is kneeling by my bed of death?

And innocence is closing up my eyes?
BOWED EYEBROWS
SILENT LIPS
BLANK PAPER
FOREVER DISCONNECTION
HATE OR UPSET
"I will consider all of the above as your love" "

The Reply Is Awaited

To My Stars...

To my stars; Eshaan, Bharti, Minshu, Aakansh, Yogita and Yuvraaj.

We all have friends, and we all ken that there are sundry categories of friends. Some friends are for life and never leave you in any situation, even if they have all the reasons to, some friends edify you a lot in life, some friends ascertain you do well in life and support you like a child and some are there to visually perceive you grow and just be blissful introverts. The type of friends I have got in my life is a coalescence of all. They'll visually perceive me tripping over a minor stone and laugh their heart out before availing and they'll withal be there if I crib about current life situations.

My friend circle has a spectrum just like the one you optically discern in rainbows. From more tenebrous to lighter shades, but here shades mean their contribution to my life. We all want to be someone's friend for life, mine have proven it an exorbitant amount of and at an exorbitant quantity of times. They'll push me to work harder and will get me presents too if I do well.

You don't operate your friends, sometimes your destiny does that for you. They come into your life as a mystical enchantment, avail you all the way, and will sit in the last row when it comes to taking credits. The munificent type of profound appreciation is what makes a companionship more vigorous than ever which is never communicated between all of us, but we ken it subsists. The best of friends don't ask for anything except authentic life skills of surviving in any condition whether biking in arctic weather or victualing sultry pabulum in the summer afternoon. We all deserve friends who make us a more jubilant person when circumvented by them in any situation, and at the same time, we should additionally endeavor to be the friend we operate in our lives.

The Lockdown Nostalgia

What a sad sadness
What a strange feeling in my heart
Neither we meet nor can we see the way
Then why did this question arise in the heart?
Why do you feel like seeing
that you are the one whose heart seeks
Why are you so beautiful?
got what he wanted
have an affinity
don't know where it will be
Let this heart sing your tune
and you still don't know
It has happened now.
I stand by your message
For those who come, there is immense happiness
If it's too late
A different restlessness in the waking heart
And if it doesn't come then just !!!

Maybe

Maybe one day we will know why we didn't get along with our parents or our relatives. Maybe we were meant to go out and make some new friends and find people who teach us that we don't have to share the same blood to count as family. Maybe we were meant to get lost and wander to find where we truly belong to find a home we don't want to escape from.

Maybe we were meant to be laughed at so we can understand that one person's tragedy is another person's comedy.

Maybe we were meant to sail away from the shore to learn the methods of surviving alone, to learn that loneliness won't kill us and solitude can be our friend sometimes.

Maybe we need to disappear to see who will care to find us, who will care to bring us back to life, who will wonder about us, and who will wish we never find our way back.

Maybe we were meant to fall in love to learn that love doesn't discriminate. That the heart doesn't know the rules or the terms of social conduct.

Maybe we need to be scared so we can understand that we will never be fearless.

What Is The Meaning Of It All?

I wonder if you'd cast a new love affair or take someone else away. I already have lost so many dead or undead souls and they all take a part of me, and I am left with almost nothing.

I now realize I live the life of "The Truman show", and I still don't hate you for controlling me, like Truman did in the movie by breaking out of the fake set his whole life was spent in.

Perhaps some of us get what you're doing and they challenge you exactly like Truman. Perhaps that's why they commit suicide to break free.

All the people who know me think that I have never in my life questioned you!

I do, and it is - "What is the meaning of it all?"

Pessimistic Beauty

I wake to the sound of your voice and I didn't find you
here for a minute,
I Was happy about it but when I realized that it was
just a dream, a dream that will not come true.
But I don't let the dream make me so sad about it,
because there's a beauty in this sadness as it reminded me
of your scent – The perfume you wore. The way you
smiled, the color of your skin, and how it shone in the sun.
It reminded me of you.
And how can such a thing make me sad?
Yes, there's beauty in sadness.

We're Blessed

We're blessed
If we see the sun every day.
We're blessed
If this global warming
We can still breathe
in the fresh air.
We're blessed if
yesterday you thought
"I will do this tomorrow"
and you wake up today
and actually
saw tomorrow becoming today.
We're blessed,
So why aren't we grateful?

Love Or Logic?

Love is the opposite of Logic.
Love is argumentative, aggressive upon the mind, and splits the world into right and wrong, us and them.
Love is generative, compassionate, and embracing all creation.
Logic pays attention to how things are said.
Logic leads to debate.
Love leads to Communion.
Practice love to be closer to humanity.

Nostalgia

It's been so long since I have heard
your voice.
When you'd speak, I imagined that's
how angles sounded like.
Every word was like a song, a beautiful
symphony.
It's been so long since I touched your lips
with mine.
The plumpness of your lips when
They touched mine and felt like
I am drinking an elixir of God.
You asked me why am I nervous
Whenever I am talking to you
Believe me, you're the only one that
Makes me feel that way.
I am another version of myself when
I am around you, uncomfortable but
Still wanting to be there.

Ending!

Heating arguments turned into a march
Involving mates and that's all you got.
Many half-hour discussions still fought.
One is beginning to cry out of helplessness.
The other one hides behind the "lying and
manipulating" art.

About The Author

Shobhit Niranjan

Shobhit Niranjan is a 20-year-old student who is currently pursuing his under graduation from the prestigious University of Delhi.

Some people understand the truth of life even before their age. Shobhit is one of them. Life is a world of dreams. There are complaints and pride in these dreams as well. We spend our lives keeping our pride in the palm. But have we ever thought that the people who were never ours, then why are we angry with them?

The reason for writing this book is to make people aware of this truth of life. Currently, Shobhit is about to end his college and is on the verge of writing another book **"The Absurd Love".**

9 798889 864721

Printed by Libri Plureos GmbH in Hamburg, Germany